Harnessing Social Media for Personal Finance Success

Table of Contents

1. Introduction 2

2. Understanding the Intersection of Social Media and Personal Finance 3

   2.1. The Advent of Social Media in Personal Finance 3

   2.2. The Impact of Social Media on Personal Finance 4

   2.3. The Role of Social Media in Financial Decision Making 4

   2.4. The Evolution of Personal Finance Paradigm in the Social Media Age 5

   2.5. The Future: Personal Finance and Social Media 6

3. Creating a Goal-Oriented Personal Finance Strategy 7

   3.1. The Importance of Setting Financial Goals 7

   3.2. Smart Financial Goals 7

   3.3. Leveraging Social Media for Strategies 8

   3.4. Incorporating Budgeting 8

   3.5. Debt Reduction Strategy 8

   3.6. Invest Wisely 9

   3.7. Establish an Emergency Fund 9

   3.8. Review and Adapt Regularly 9

4. Identifying Reliable Finance Influencers and Resources 10

   4.1. The Role of a Finance Influencer 10

   4.2. Criteria for Identifying Reliable Influencers 10

   4.3. Platforms Hosting Finance Influencers 11

   4.4. Discerning Reliable Online Finance Resources 11

   4.5. Keeping Bias in Check 12

   4.6. Fact-Checking Information 12

   4.7. Monitor the Evolution of Influential Voices 12

5. Utilizing Social Media to Improve Financial Literacy 13

   5.1. Recognizing the Immeasurable Worth of Social Media 13

5.2. Levelling Up Your Financial Acumen with Social Media 14

5.3. Actively Participating in Online Finance Communities 14

5.4. Being Savvy About Social Media Scams 15

5.5. The Promise and Power of Social Media 15

6. Popular Social Media Platforms for Financial Education 17

6.1. Twitter as a Financial Education Hub 17

6.2. LinkedIn's Role in Professional Financial Guidance 18

6.3. Instagram – A Pictorial Guide to Finance 18

6.4. YouTube – Multifaceted Financial Learning 19

6.5. Reddit – The Power of Community 19

7. Cautions and Pitfalls: Avoiding Online Financial Scams 21

7.1. Introduction to Online Financial Scams 21

7.2. Recognising Different Types of Online Financial Scams 21

7.3. The Role of Social Media in Online Financial Scams 22

7.4. Exposing Common Social Media Scam Tactics 22

7.5. Building Your Defence: How to Avoid Online Financial

Scams 22

7.6. Reporting and Recovering from Online Financial Scams 23

7.7. A Case Study of a Successful Scam and Its Aftermath 23

7.8. Conclusion: Staying a Step Ahead of the Scammers 23

8. Online Investment Opportunities: Using Social Media as a

Guide 25

8.1. Identifying Social Media Channels 25

8.2. Curation of Content 26

8.3. Understanding Market Trends and Investment Tips 26

8.4. Education and Professional Guidance 27

8.5. Embracing Robo-advisors and Fintech Solutions 27

9. Crowdfunding and Peer-to-Peer Lending: Capitalizing on Social

Financial Opportunities 29

9.1. Crowdfunding: The Basics 29

9.2. Peer-To-Peer Lending: Cutting Out The Middleman 30

9.3. Capitalizing on Social Financial Opportunities 30

9.4. Crowdfunding and P2P Lending: Proceed with Caution 31

10. Leveraging Virtual Networking for Financial Success 33

10.1. Using your Network Effectively 33

10.2. Building your Personal Brand 33

10.3. Virtual Networking Events 34

10.4. Utilizing Online Financial Communities and Forums 34

10.5. Tapping into the Gig Economy 35

10.6. Innovatively Leveraging Professional Networks 35

10.7. Conclusion 35

11. Case Studies: Success Stories in Harnessing Social Media for
Personal Finance 36

11.1. The Experts' Stories 36

11.2. Empowering the Everyday Individual 37

11.3. Enterprises Benefitting from Social Media 38

Wealth is not about having a lot of money; it's about having a lot of options.

Chapter 1. Introduction

In an increasingly digitized world, your path to financial triumph could be just a few clicks away! This thrilling Special Report titled "Harnessing Social Media for Personal Finance Success" is designed to help you navigate the bustling avenues of social media platforms to boost your financial stability and growth. Our report isn't just a guide, it's your stepping stone to personal wealth, leveraging the prowess of platforms you use every day. By casting the mysteries of personal finance in a practical, easy-to-understand narrative, we're offering you a roadmap to successfully manoeuvre financial hurdles. We promise to enlighten, to motivate, and to transform your financial journey. Get ready to embark on an empowering expedition into personal finance, made fun and accessible through the engaging realm of social media. Enrich your life and secure your future today, one post, share and tweet at a time!

Chapter 2. Understanding the Intersection of Social Media and Personal Finance

Stepping into the contemporary landscape of personal finance, it's apparent that the traditional modes of financial management are gradually being replaced, or at least supplemented, by social media. This revolutionary change is not a mere accident or by-product of the digital age but is largely shaped by the fundamentally transformative role that these platforms play in curating, sharing, and acting upon financial information. Let's delve deeper into this subject and understand why and how this intersection matters to you.

2.1. The Advent of Social Media in Personal Finance

The engagement of social media in personal finance did not occur overnight. It was a steady progression pioneered by the emergence of the Internet. Following this, foresightful entrepreneurs began establishing online businesses, taking advantage of the extensive connectivity. As the World Wide Web became more user-friendly over the years, social media platforms surfaced and rapidly gained popularity due to their interactive nature, intuitive design, and inherent potential for wide-scale networking. These platforms drastically changed how information is consumed, disseminating financial content exponentially.

This accessibility, coupled with the unfiltered and instantaneous mode of information sharing, sparked a 'socialization' of personal finance. Savvy users rapidly perceived the potential of these platforms as tools for effective communication, networking, and knowledge gain, thereby pioneering the integration of social media into contemporary personal finance practices.

2.2. The Impact of Social Media on Personal Finance

The impact of social media on personal finance is twofold: It democratizes financial knowledge and alters trends in personal finance.

It's now seamlessly possible for anyone, regardless of their financial background, to access valuable insights and learn from seasoned professionals through platforms such as Facebook, LinkedIn, Twitter, and Instagram. These platforms host a vast array of influencers, finance gurus, and companies that share tips, tricks, and advice addressing various financial topics, from saving and investing to budgeting and financial planning. This freely accessible financial advice provides empowerment to individuals, encouraging proactive financial management.

Moreover, social media platforms play a crucial role in constantly shape-shifting the trends in personal finance. Pervasive platforms like Instagram, Twitter, or TikTok turn into stages where novel financial strategies, concepts, or products are introduced and popularized. Social media acts as a powerful influencer in forming public opinion about different financial vehicles, affecting how individuals perceive and utilize them.

2.3. The Role of Social Media in Financial Decision Making

Social media platforms have a profound impact on participants' financial decision-making processes. Users can track their financial heroes, align their financial goals, and embark on investment journeys, mimicking strategies and steps that resonate with them.

However, navigation in this realm comes with its perils. One must not forget the presence of misinformation and unverified advice on these platforms. The democratization of information also means that anyone, regardless of their expertise, can disseminate financial advice. Careful discernment is needed to sieve through the enormous amount of data exchanged daily. A sound strategy involves cross-verifying information with credible, reliable sources, tapping into a variety of perspectives while simultaneously mastering the fine art of skepticism.

2.4. The Evolution of Personal Finance Paradigm in the Social Media Age

The integration of personal finance into social media hasn't merely caused an evolutionary shift; in many ways, it has caused a paradigm shift—a significant change in an individual's concept and practice of managing personal finance.

Where finance management was once perceived as a private activity—one that happened behind closed doors—it has now moved into the public sphere. This transition is marked by heightened levels of transparency, availability of peer-to-peer advice, and a community approach to financial problem-solving.

With such a shift, collaboration has become a fundamental element of personal finance management. Online communities, groups, and forums make it possible for individuals to discuss financial topics, share experiences, give advice, and learn from one other's successes and failures.

In a nutshell, the fusion of personal finance with social media has shaped an engaged, informed, collaborative financial culture. And while caution is necessary, the benefits of harnessing social media for better financial control and growth are undeniable.

2.5. The Future: Personal Finance and Social Media

As long as social media platforms continue to thrive and innovate, their link with personal finance will persist and intensify. Future intersections could take unexpected paths due to advances in technology and shifts in societal norms. Potential future trends might involve further customization of financial advice through advanced AI algorithms, increasing prevalence of personal finance influencers, and perhaps even stricter regulations concerning financial advice on social media platforms.

The intersection of personal finance and social media is an evolving phenomenon, propelled by technological advent and adaptive users. Those who are willing to understand and harness the capabilities of this dynamic intersection stand to gain a significant advantage in managing, growing, and protecting their wealth.

To embark on this journey towards financial triumph, an open mind, constant learning, and prudent decision-making hone the key. As we traverse through the ebbs and flows of this intersection, we create our narrative in the vast saga of personal finance. Onward, then, to a more mindful, informed, and enriched financial future!

Chapter 3. Creating a Goal-Oriented Personal Finance Strategy

In order to achieve financial prosperity, it is essential to develop a strategic plan tailored to your personal financial goals. This systematic initiative, powered by conscious thought, will guide you in making informed decisions that positively impact your wealth journey.

3.1. The Importance of Setting Financial Goals

Setting financial goals is of paramount importance on your road to financial success. Whether it's buying a home, saving for retirement, or achieving financial independence, outlining specific, concrete goals sets you on a path that allows you to make a holistic plan. It provides you the motivation and direction needed to make wise financial decisions. Social media platforms can be beneficial in this endeavor, presenting easier access to financial advisors, influencers, and other individuals who provide a wealth of valuable insights and motivation.

3.2. Smart Financial Goals

SMART, an acronym for Specific, Measurable, Attainable, Realistic, and Time-bound, is a proven strategy utilized in various realms, especially personal finance. Social media platforms can aid in shaping SMART financial goals. You can find resources, influencers, and personal success stories demonstrating how to set SMART goals. Leveraging these resources, you should clearly detail your financial targets, identifying the sum you aim to achieve, setting realistic timelines, and frequently monitoring your progress.

3.3. Leveraging Social Media for Strategies

A sea of knowledge, experience and advice resides on social media platforms. Leveraging these resources, you can develop financial strategies that resonate with your goals. From savings techniques, debt reduction strategies, or investment advice, social media provides an extensively broad palate of resources to enhance your financial strategies. However, always ensure verifying the credibility of the advice or resource utilized.

3.4. Incorporating Budgeting

Structuring a budget is the cornerstone of personal finance. This tool brings clarity to your income, expenses and helps streamline your financial behavior towards your objective. Social media can offer multiple innovative budgeting techniques, templates, and insights, enabling you to design an easy-to-follow and efficient budget. Moreover, a plethora of apps and tools shared on these platforms can be used to automate the budgeting process, enabling you to track your expenses effectively.

3.5. Debt Reduction Strategy

Mounting debts can slow your financial pursuit. Nodes of information on social media can provide you with expert advice regarding strategies to pay off debts swiftly. Here, you can find detailed articles, podcasts, and videos narrated by financial experts that talk about techniques like debt snowballing or debt avalanching.

3.6. Invest Wisely

Investing implies utilizing your money to earn profits continually. Social media platforms host numerous financial influencers and professionals who frequently share their financial acumen and insights around various investment avenues, suitable per different personal finance objectives. Such platforms are a remarkable source of knowledge for beginner investors, offering insights into stocks, bonds, mutual funds, real estate, and more.

3.7. Establish an Emergency Fund

Unforeseen expenditures may arise anytime and could create a financial havoc if not prepared. An emergency fund acts as the safety net for such scenarios. Social media can motivate you in shaping such a fund, offering support, guidance, and shared experiences as to why, how much, and how the emergency fund should be constructed.

3.8. Review and Adapt Regularly

The finance ecosystem continually evolves, thus, reviewing and adapting your strategy is pivotal. From changing economic conditions, varied risk tolerance, or altered financial objectives, your directorial strategy should be flexible. Social media can update you on the financial world's novelties, enabling you to refine your strategy accordingly.

In conclusion, social media yields countless resources, tools, and experts that aid in creating a personalized, goal-oriented financial strategy. By harnessing this power, you equip yourself with knowledge and insights, making your financial expedition less intimidating, more comprehendible, and achievable. Remember, social media, when used consciously, can be the ladder to your financial triumph, one share, one post, one tweet at a time.

Chapter 4. Identifying Reliable Finance Influencers and Resources

Navigating the vast digital landscape of personal finance can be a daunting endeavour. The key to utilize these online tools effectively lies in identifying the right influencers and resources that offer accurate, comprehensive, and actionable financial insight. These figures provide a wealth of knowledge, helping individuals craft personal finance plans, make informed investment decisions, and simply get better at managing money.

4.1. The Role of a Finance Influencer

Often, financial influencers are experts in their field, offering insights borne by years of experience and broad market understanding. They deliberate on various aspects of personal finance, including budgeting, saving, investing, retirement planning, and more. Armed with a forceful online presence, their words often permeate the bulk of the personal finance community. They have an immediate and tremendous impact, affecting how we understand and manage our finances. However, it is crucial to realize that not all influencers are created equal; some provide insightful, value-laden content while others serve as mere talking heads.

4.2. Criteria for Identifying Reliable Influencers

When identifying reliable finance influencers, one must consider their credentials, the authenticity of their content, how well they engage with their audiences, whether they provide actionable advice, and their approach to handling financial risks. These, coupled with consistent output, a significant following, and a high engagement rate, often distinguish credible influencers from their less dependable counterparts.

4.3. Platforms Hosting Finance Influencers

Social media platforms such as Instagram, Twitter, LinkedIn, YouTube and Facebook are teeming with finance influencers, each with their unique value proposition. For instance, YouTube hosts a plethora of educational video content that presents complex financial concepts in a digestible manner. Financial bloggers populate Twitter and Instagram with insights and news, whereas LinkedIn is home to more professionally geared financial content, including thought leadership articles and white papers.

4.4. Discerning Reliable Online Finance Resources

Apart from influencers, there exist a wealth of online resources dedicated to personal finance; these include finance blogs, podcasts, online forums, newsletters, webinars, e-books, and financial apps. All these tools can augment your understanding of personal finance, but the challenge lies in discerning which resources are accurate and reliable.

When evaluating these platforms, check the source's credentials, analyse the quality and tone of the content, examine the community engagement, and make sure the information provided aligns with proven financial practices.

4.5. Keeping Bias in Check

While social media offers a wealth of financial wisdom, one must remember that the platform also runs rampant with personal bias. It's crucial to approach the information with a critical eye, mindfully navigating through the sea of varying opinions. Any advice should be evaluated against a backdrop of personal financial objectives and macroeconomic contexts before being implemented.

4.6. Fact-Checking Information

Ensure that the information provided by an influencer or resource undergoes rigorous verification. Cross-reference with other reliable sources, consult with professional advisors or utilize fact-checking websites. Remember, your financial future hinges on informed decisions birthed from accurate information.

4.7. Monitor the Evolution of Influential Voices

The digital marketplace of ideas is dynamic, with influencers and resources constantly emerging and evolving. As such, users must remain updated, attentive to shifts in paradigms, changes in financial thought leadership, and the emergence of new authoritative voices.

In conclusion, the secret to harnessing the power of social media for personal finance success lies partly in identifying reliable finance influencers and resources. This process implies understanding what makes a credible influencer and resource, discerning platform-specific nuances, and employing effective strategies to manage bias and validate content. The goal remains to cultivate financial literacy and stability, a task made more accessible by the efficient navigation of the social media landscape. It is a journey of education and growth – a ceaseless endeavour of financial empowerment.

Chapter 5. Utilizing Social Media to Improve Financial Literacy

Financial literacy does not spring up overnight. It involves a learning process, a perpetual scrutiny of trends, data, and advice. One powerful tool to support this progression is indeed social media. These online platforms can undoubtedly help you acquire practical knowledge and boost your personal finance skills, assuming you know where to look and whom to follow.

5.1. Recognizing the Immeasurable Worth of Social Media

The charm of social media is multifaceted. Its inherent knack to foster connectivity and communication at impressive speeds makes it a valuable adjunct in your quest for financial literacy. This potential is compounded by the richness of content, where discussions range from basic budgeting tips to advanced investment strategies, all of which lend themselves to a well-rounded, comprehensive financial education.

On top of this, there are numerous online communities focused solely on personal finance. These vibrant groups constitute a broad demographic of individuals, from budding entrepreneurs and seasoned investors to people downright curious about wealth management and savings.

Though daunting due to the sheer volume of information, once tamed, social media is an unparalleled resource. It's a dynamic knowledge bank that continues to expand with the collective wisdom of its users.

5.2. Levelling Up Your Financial Acumen with Social Media

To successfully leverage social media for financial literacy, you'll need to be strategic. Start by aligning your social media consumption with your financial goals. Each platform has its strengths. For instance, YouTube offers detailed video tutorials and webinars, LinkedIn hosts thought leaders and industry professionals, while Instagram and TikTok are a hub for creative, bite-sized educational content.

Ensure your chosen content is provided by credible sources. Look for certified financial planners, well-respected finance bloggers, or influential personalities with proven financial acumen. They should offer balanced views grounded in expertise and experience, not driven by product bias or promotion.

Some notable figures worth following include: * Suze Orman, author and TV host known for her personal finance advice * Dave Ramsey, famous for his ideology of a debt-free life * Robert Kiyosaki, best-selling author of Rich Dad Poor Dad. Parsing their content can provide multifaceted, expert insights about wealth management, budgeting, and investment.

5.3. Actively Participating in Online Finance Communities

Online finance communities are a treasure trove of knowledge. Interactive, encouraging, and resource-rich, these virtual spaces offer a comfortable environment for learning. Platforms like Reddit are replete with such active communities including subreddits like r/personalfinance and r/investing.

These platforms are no mere spectator sport. Actively engaging in discussions, posing questions, sharing experiences, and responding to queries can significantly contribute to your learning. Remember to be respectful and open-minded, recognizing that every individual's financial landscape is unique.

5.4. Being Savvy About Social Media Scams

Harnessing the power of social media for financial literacy is a double-edged sword. While it offers immense learning potential, it can also be used nefariously. Scam artists, fraudsters, and false information purveyors lurk in the corners of every platform, ready to compromise your nascent financial journey.

Take no information at face value, especially when it promises fast returns with no risk. Verify sources, challenge too-good-to-be-true predictions, and shy away from any solicitation that pressures for immediate action. Reaching out to a mentor or financial advisor in such scenarios could be a saving grace.

5.5. The Promise and Power of Social Media

In the age of the digital economy, social media sits at the nexus of personal finance and education, espousing a culture that values financial literacy. It's a gold mine of information and knowledge, ripe to be utilized as a potent weapon against financial illiteracy.

By embracing social media, you're not only investing in your financial future but also contributing to a wider societal movement toward financial empowerment. The journey to financial literacy may require time and diligence, with social media acting as a supportive aide, amplifying your learning curve.

Remember, your financial literacy journey on social media is wholly yours to design. Take it in strides, as even the most successful investors had to begin somewhere, picking up pearls of wisdom along their path. That's the beauty of continuous learning, and the role that social media can play.

Chapter 6. Popular Social Media Platforms for Financial Education

With the proliferation of social media and its boundless influence on our everyday lives, it's no surprise that these platforms have become invaluable tools for acquiring financial knowledge. These highly interactive mediums not only facilitate the dissemination of vital keynotes on smart money management but also host a plethora of engaging dialogues, potent tools, and resources to aid your educational journey. Whether you're a neophyte getting your bearings or a financially savvy individual seeking to expand your knowledge, there's a platform designed to meet your unique needs. This chapter elucidates in exhaustive detail the popular social media platforms that are gaining acclaim for the significant roles they play in financial education.

6.1. Twitter as a Financial Education Hub

Twitter, the go-to platform for real-time updates on a diversity of topics, rises as a great place to discover advice, motivational tips, and insights from financial experts. With a simple search using financial hashtags like #PersonalFinance, #Investing, or #FinancialAdvice, you can float down a river of relevant, up-to-the-minute information. Additionally, you can choose to follow financial influencers or organizations that post bite-sized financial advice, various perspectives on current market trends and education on investment strategies on regular intervals.

However, in the clamour of the Twitterverse, it's crucial to verify the credibility of the sources. Cross-check the qualifications and expertise of the influencers or organizations before taking their advice at face value. It's also easy to get lost in the fast-paced stream of incoming tweets and retweets, so be selective in who you follow to ensure that your Twitter feed remains an enriching, clutter-free font of information.

6.2. LinkedIn's Role in Professional Financial Guidance

For those seeking a more professional slant, LinkedIn is the ideal platform to explore. Renowned for fostering professional contacts and career development, this platform also serves as a treasured trove of financial knowledge. Career-driven individuals, business owners, and entrepreneurs regularly post informative articles, provide insights, and share experiences pertaining to sound financial management from a business perspective.

The LinkedIn Learning platform offers a variety of courses, ranging from basic financial literacy to more complex topics such as fiscal strategy, financial modelling, and more. The use of groups also offers concentrated forums where users can pose queries, exchange views, and share resources. Use the platform's robust search functionality to find groups relevant to your financial objectives.

6.3. Instagram – A Pictorial Guide to Finance

Instagram, a platform synonymous with captivating visuals, is not just about selfies and aesthetic travel views but it's also a rich source of engaging, straightforward financial advice. Instagram's power lies in its ability to render complex financial concepts into digestible, visually engaging content. Finance-centric pages often employ colourful infographics, short videos, and creative carousels to cover a range of financial topics.

Still, caution is key. Instagram's focus on aesthetics should not overshadow the quality and source credibility of financial advice presented. Like any other platform, ensure the information you gather comes from reputable sources and takes into account your personal financial situation before acting upon any advice.

6.4. YouTube – Multifaceted Financial Learning

YouTube, with its in-depth visual content, undeniably provides a comprehensive approach towards personal finance. At the core of its utility is the wide variety of video content on nearly every financial topic conceivable. From simple 'how-to' guides explaining the basics of budgeting and saving to intricate discourses on macroeconomic trends and investment strategies, YouTube houses a wealth of knowledge.

You can subscribe to channels curated by finance experts or institutions for a structured learning journey, or sample a variety of channels to broaden your perspective. YouTube's sophistication lies in its ability to provide content matching the pace, style, and depth of instruction that resonates uniquely with you. Keep in mind, though, that the platform's usability as a finance tool is proportional to your discernment — subscribe to channels proven for their expertise and accuracy.

6.5. Reddit – The Power of Community

Over the years, Reddit has emerged as an unconventional yet highly beneficial resource for finance. The platform's finance-related subreddits such as r/personalfinance, r/investing, and r/financialindependence function as active discussion boards where users ranging from financial novices to expert investors share insights, seek advice, discuss news and strategies, and learn from real-world experiences.

This platform's charm lies in its democratic nature, where the community drives content generation and curation. Every post or comment can be upvoted or downvoted, ensuring the quality content rises to the top. However, immense care should be taken to comprehend that while some advice may be beneficial, not all of it may be accurate or appropriate for your specific circumstances.

In conclusion, the choice of social media platforms for financial education is vast and diverse, and the information quite exhaustive. These platforms, when used judiciously, can become potent instruments in your journey of financial conquest. Remember to be discerning, cross-check information, and adapt the knowledge gained to fit your unique financial context. By doing so, you unlock the true educational potential of these platforms, leading the way to informed financial choices and successful wealth-building strategies.

Chapter 7. Cautions and Pitfalls: Avoiding Online Financial Scams

In the shimmering digital marketplace of 24/7 financial transactions, opportunities and risks go hand in hand. The internet's interconnected nature, so advantageous for information flow, can also become a haven for financial scams, promising golden returns but delivering ruin instead. Unveiling the best practices to avoid such scams, we embark on an investigative journey, making sense of the pitfalls lurking behind every click, like and share.

7.1. Introduction to Online Financial Scams

Online financial scams have proliferated in the digital age. They take on many forms, from Ponzi schemes promising high returns on investments, to fake charity drives manipulating your goodwill. Scammers exploit the anonymity provided by the internet and employ sophisticated ways to deceive unsuspecting victims. Recognising these scams is the first defence against them. But this is just the start.

7.2. Recognising Different Types of Online Financial Scams

Informed recognition of scams is vital for protection. This will encompass a review of common scam varieties. For example, 'get-rich-quick' schemes that tempt your ambition, phishing expeditions that aim to steal sensitive financial data, or investment opportunities wrapped in enterprising but non-existent projects. Recognising the extensive vocabulary of scams empowers the online user with critical scepticism.

7.3. The Role of Social Media in Online Financial Scams

A significant platform that scammers employ is social media. The platform's accessibility and wide reach, coupled with users' trust, generates a fertile ground for scams. Scammers impersonate trustworthy entities, establish fake profiles, or even exploit existing connections to deceive victims. Here, the intersection of social comfort and financial vulnerability requires special attention.

7.4. Exposing Common Social Media Scam Tactics

Armed with the knowledge of how scams operate, we unravel the tactics used on social media. These include exclusive investment opportunities, appeals for help, lottery or contest scams, and cloning or impersonating profiles. By understanding these tactics, you'll be equipped to outsmart even the craftiest scam.

7.5. Building Your Defence: How to Avoid Online Financial Scams

Realising the diversity of online scams, let's build a solid defence strategy. This covers verifying the authenticity of profiles and financial opportunities, critically assessing requests for sensitive information, and maintaining updated digital security measures. Diligent application of these principles can provide a robust shield against scams.

7.6. Reporting and Recovering from Online Financial Scams

Even with the best strategies in place, it's important to have a plan if you fall victim to a scam. We delve into procedures to report scams and steps for recovering, as much as possible, from the losses incurred. Prompt and appropriate response to scams is crucial in minimising damages, and deterring future scam attempts.

7.7. A Case Study of a Successful Scam and Its Aftermath

To illustrate the true nature of scams and their destructive power, we delve into a detailed case study. This saga of deception and fall underscores the importance of the strategies discussed above, while laying bare the ruthless execution employed by scammers.

7.8. Conclusion: Staying a Step Ahead of the Scammers

The online financial landscape, peppered with scams, may seem treacherous. However, insurmountable as they may feel, scams can be outsmarted. Let's affirm the defensive measures discussed, reminding ourselves of the teachings encapsulated in our case study. Mitigating the risk of scams is a continuous process, and being persistent in our vigilance, we can stay a step ahead of the scammers and pave our path to financial success.

To truly harness the advantages of social media for personal finance, understanding scams and implementing protective measures is crucial. In the following chapter, we will explore online investment opportunities and learn how to use social media, not just to protect our wealth, but to enhance it. Let's stride confidently into the digital future, armed with knowledge and vigilant in enforcement.

Chapter 8. Online Investment Opportunities: Using Social Media as a Guide

Taking the digital leap and delving into online investment opportunities can present itself as a daunting task. Where do you start, and whom to trust? Luckily, in an era of social media, the vast troves of information readily available to us can guide us through the labyrinth of investment opportunities. However, discerning high-quality content from misinformation is quintessential. This chapter provides a comprehensive guide to navigating the abundant resources on social media platforms concerning online investment opportunities.

8.1. Identifying Social Media Channels

Firstly, it's essential to identify and familiarize yourself with the various social media channels that offer insights on investment opportunities. LinkedIn is often a fantastic place to start, a platform where professionals from finance, including traders, analysts, and investment advisors share their insights. Discussion groups on LinkedIn often house a trove of information on emerging trends and potential investment opportunities.

On the other hand, Twitter is teeming with thought leaders and influential personalities in the finance world who share breaking news, trends, and personal opinions on investment avenues. Besides, online forums like Reddit host a myriad of threads discussing investments, where you can draw insight from other users' experiences.

Lastly, YouTube provides an array of learning resources, from basics to pro-level investing tips explained through video content. Influencers and financial gurus regularly post videos to educate their subscribers and share investment opportunities they've found successful.

8.2. Curation of Content

Once you've identified available channels, the next step is curating your content. The most critical aspect of content curation is following the right accounts; finance professionals, investment companies, financial news outlets, and other industry players can deliver reliable and up-to-date information. This helps you stay informed on market trends and investment opportunities, but remember that it is vital to cross-check information and get a second opinion, always.

Joining relevant groups and participating in discussions related to your areas of interest or investment can also be beneficial. On Twitter, hashtags can guide you towards information pertaining to specific investments. Similarly, subreddits on Reddit can be used to find threads about diverse and specialized investment topics.

8.3. Understanding Market Trends and Investment Tips

Another vital thing to remember is that social media platforms are also excellent tools for understanding current market trends. Experts regularly post detailed analyses offering in-depth insights into market sectors, which can provide a solid understanding of the state of the market in general, as well as specific investment prospects.

Investment tips are another helpful resource plentiful on social media. However, always exercise caution and ensure any 'tips' originated from trusted and vetted sources to avoid falling prey to unscrupulous individuals or organizations out to manipulate stock prices or investment decisions.

8.4. Education and Professional Guidance

Many financial experts maintain active social media profiles, choosing to disseminate knowledge to their followers. Blogs, podcasts, webinars, online courses - social media has democratized access to financial education. Look for financial planners or advisors who offer webinars and online tutorials about investing on social media platforms.

Some even offer Q&A sessions for followers, helping address specific queries and provide personalized advice. Meanwhile, online investment courses discussed via social media channels enable you to master new skills and keep abreast of developments in the finance world.

8.5. Embracing Robo-advisors and Fintech Solutions

With the advent of Fintech solutions, Robo-advisors have been making waves in the investment sector. Social media platforms, particularly LinkedIn, often host discussions concerning these emerging technologies, and audiences can gain insights into how best to harness them for their investing strategy.

Robo-advisors, for example, provide automatic portfolio management services, making them a popular choice among neophyte investors. Utilizing such platforms discussed in social media can augment your investing strategy by providing additional diversification, automatic rebalancing, and algorithms that optimize for tax benefits.

In conclusion, social media platforms can provide an abundance of information regarding online investment opportunities. This information, when suitably harnessed and critically analyzed, can significantly enhance your financial journey. Cautiously recognize the potential of these tools and verify the credibility and accuracy of the information obtained before making any financial decisions. Your journey to financial triumph is just a click away!

Chapter 9. Crowdfunding and Peer-to-Peer Lending: Capitalizing on Social Financial Opportunities

In the vibrant digital finance ecosystem, one trend is clear: while traditional financing methods still have their place, the rise of crowdfunding and peer-to-peer lending represent exciting new avenues for funding and investment. These avenues offer tremendous potential for personal finance development by leveraging the collective economic power of the masses. Compounded by the vast reach of social media, these opportunities introduce innovative ways to improve and diversify your fiscal portfolio.

9.1. Crowdfunding: The Basics

Crowdfunding is a promising new player in the arena of finance, championed by the power of social media connectivity and accessibility. At its core, crowdfunding is a modern method for funding a venture, be it personal, entrepreneurial or charitable, through small amounts of money received from a large number of individuals, usually via the Internet. Inspired individuals or groups can articulate their goals, pitch their ideas, and solicit funds from a diverse global audience, transforming passive social media users into proactive contributors and investors. This democratises finance, empowering people to partake in ventures they believe in and inspiring a sense of community and camaraderie.

Whether you're funding your startup, supporting a community project, or furthering a personal goal, crowdfunding platforms like Kickstarter, Indiegogo, and GoFundMe, among others, serve as conduits between your dream and potential backers from around the world. The effectiveness of crowdfunding lies in its ability to communicate a compelling narrative to a vast audience, turn sympathisers into supporters, and dreamers into doers.

9.2. Peer-To-Peer Lending: Cutting Out The Middleman

Moving from crowdfunding, let's delve into peer-to-peer (P2P) lending, a disruptor that's been giving traditional banking systems a run for their money. No longer are we beholden to banks and credit unions for loans. With P2P lending platforms, such as LendingClub, Prosper, and Zopa, we can sidestep these institutions directly to borrow from or lend to individuals or small businesses.

Modern P2P lending platforms act as intermediaries that connect investors with borrowers, facilitating the loan process while also ensuring security measures and checks. The streamlined process and the enhanced personal relationship between investor and borrower have made this form of finance increasingly popular. Moreover, the potential for better interest rates for both parties make it an attractive prospect for those looking to invest or secure a loan.

9.3. Capitalizing on Social Financial Opportunities

Already, we've seen how crowdfunding and P2P lending are revolutionizing personal finance. But how do we tap into these promising opportunities? Here's where we introduce social media, the great enabler. Social media networks such as Facebook, Twitter, LinkedIn, and Instagram, among others, have become tools to connect, engage, and persuade a global audience. They amplify our reach and influence and can be used to drive crowdfunding campaigns and enhance the visibility of P2P lending opportunities. Let's delve deeper:

- Crowdfunding campaigns can leverage social media platforms to increase visibility and funding potential. Success lies in creating an engaging narrative around the project, establishing credibility, and maintaining consistent communication with potential backers. A strategically planned social media strategy can help the campaign reach and engage a broader, more demographically diverse audience, ensuring the participation of more backers.

- Similarly, for P2P lending, social media can act as a valuable networking tool. Through smart profiling and personal branding, borrowers can establish a sense of trust and confidence among potential lenders. Similarly, lenders can keep an eye on market trends, understand popular investment avenues, and explore opportunities to diversify their lending portfolio.

9.4. Crowdfunding and P2P Lending: Proceed with Caution

While crowdfunding and P2P lending offer immense potential, it's crucial to approach with caution. Not all platforms operate the same. Some crowdfunding initiatives offer rewards or equity in return for backing, while some are donation-based. Similarly, while P2P lending can yield high returns, the risk factor is equally substantial. Therefore, establishing due diligence, understanding the platform policies, and researching the credibility of participants is crucial.

Embrace these financial innovations, conduct your due diligence, and harness the potential of social media platforms to engage with these ventures. By leveraging crowdfunding and P2P lending, you're not just investing in an idea or a project; you're investing in a community and arguably, in the future of personal finance itself.

These social financial opportunities herald a new age of democratization in finance - accessible, engaging and in step with modern digital trends.

Chapter 10. Leveraging Virtual Networking for Financial Success

In an increasingly interconnected world, utilizing the potential of virtual networks for financial success has become an indispensable strategy. This chapter explores how virtual networking can be harnessed as a tool to propel your financial prosperity. We will delve deeply into best practices and provide an insightful guide on how to use your network to maximize financial gains.

10.1. Using your Network Effectively

The foundation of leveraging virtual networking for financial success is understanding how to use your network effectively. The idea of networking often conjures up images of business meetings and formal events, but virtual networking extends beyond that. It refers to forming and fostering relationships online with individuals who can directly or indirectly contribute to your personal finance success.

Many social media platforms such as LinkedIn, Facebook, and Twitter offer vast opportunities to connect with key individuals in the areas of finance and investing. The first step in effective networking is to be proactive. Reach out to influencers, join relevant groups or forums, participate in discussions, and share engaging content that displays your interest and knowledge. Remember, networking is about building relationships before you need them.

10.2. Building your Personal Brand

In the digital age, your personal brand equals to your reputation. It's how people perceive you, your values, your capabilities, and helps to establish you as a credible authority in your chosen field. Build a solid personal brand by actively participating in online finance communities, attending virtual finance seminars and workshops, sharing insightful articles on your social media profiles, and maintaining a consistent online presence. A substantial personal brand not only attracts people to your network but can also establish you as a thought leader in the field. If you become known as a go-to expert in personal finance, job offers, investment opportunities, and collaborations may start coming your way.

10.3. Virtual Networking Events

Virtual networking events hold a unique position in the world of online networking. Attending webinars, virtual conferences, and online workshops provides an excellent opportunity to connect with like-minded individuals who are passionate about personal finance. Use these platforms to learn about new financial trends, find out valuable tips and techniques, and to expand your network by connecting with key influencers and thought leaders in the finance world.

10.4. Utilizing Online Financial Communities and Forums

When we talk about virtual networking, the role of online communities and forums cannot be overstressed. These communities are troves of information where you can ask questions, share your knowledge, and learn from experts and peers. Sites such as Reddit, Quora, or Personal Finance sub-Reddit provide an invaluable platform to engage with a wide array of financial topics. Make the most of these online resources to learn, contribute, and, eventually, lead.

10.5. Tapping into the Gig Economy

The gig economy has seen a massive surge with the rise of digital technology. With platforms like Upwork, Fiverr, or Freelancer, you can network with potential clients and industry professionals, build a strong portfolio while earning, and invest these earnings towards your financial goals.

10.6. Innovatively Leveraging Professional Networks

Professional networking sites, such as LinkedIn, can offer significant benefits to your personal finance success. By taking advantage of LinkedIn groups, you can interact with professionals, participate in insightful discussions, and stay updated with industry trends, thereby equipping yourself with market-savvy insights for financial success.

10.7. Conclusion

Leveraging virtual networking for financial success isn't intuitively straightforward, and it requires persistence and active participation. But with the methodology and platforms outlined in this chapter, you're fully equipped to begin. Remember, the key is to connect, communicate, and contribute. In doing so, you can exponentially increase your finance knowledge, broaden your perspective, and create opportunities – the essential ingredients for financial success in today's digital age.

Chapter 11. Case Studies: Success Stories in Harnessing Social Media for Personal Finance

The domain of personal finance can seem intimidating and complex to navigate for many. It is often fraught with fears of making poor decisions, lack of understanding about investment options, and overall uncertainty about how to maximize one's earnings. However, integrating social media, which offers immediate and easy access to information, into your financial management strategy can lead to monumental success. In this chapter, we delve into the intriguing success stories of numerous individuals and enterprises who employed social media platforms as tools for managing and growing their wealth.

11.1. The Experts' Stories

Let's commence our narrative with the stories of personal finance gurus who have utilized social media to not only manage their own fortunes but also teach their followers the art of financial management.

The first tale is about Edward Grant, a millennial social media influencer who set forth on his journey as a financial advisor while still a college student. He started sharing his own experiences in saving money, reducing debt, and gradually expanding his investment portfolio by posting videos on YouTube. His common-sense approach gained immediate traction. Edward's story highlights precisely how simply sharing practical advice on an accessible platform can attract a wide audience. Today, he has over a million subscribers, and his financial growth mirrors that of his follower base.

Our second protagonist holds a powerful presence on Instagram. Catherine Arnold, with a background in finance, has amassed thousands of followers on the platform. By sharing visually appealing infographics and snippets of financial wisdom in her posts and stories, she has managed to make personal finance appealing and understandable for an extensive audience demographic. Her online activities have not only improved her personal finances, primarily through sponsored content and collaborations but have guided her diverse followers towards their financial goals too.

11.2. Empowering the Everyday Individual

Moving on to stories featuring ordinary individuals like you and me who have used social media to enhance their personal finances. Their narratives emphasize that one doesn't need to be a financial expert or influencer to benefit from social media's reach.

Our first narrative takes us to Carla Johnson, a single mother who stumbled upon a Facebook group that focused on financial independence. By conferring with the group regularly and assimilating the financial strategies shared, Carla managed to climb out of debt within a couple of years. She also started investing in retirement funds, stocks, and real estate, thanks to the connections and resources she found on the platform.

The story of Neil Patel, a freelance graphic designer active on LinkedIn, further illustrates the power of social media. Neil used the platform to connect with potential clients, establishing a robust global clientele. He also joined several groups dedicated to financial planning for freelancers. Learning from shared resources and interacting with other members helped Neil develop a comprehensive financial plan to manage his fluctuating income, enabling him to create an emergency fund, health coverage, and a retirement savings plan.

11.3. Enterprises Benefitting from Social Media

Lastly, we peruse the landscape of businesses that have used social media to drive their financial success, proving that social media can significantly impact an organization's fiscal health.

One such business is a small local bakery operating in Portland, Oregon. Aware of the power social networks hold, the owner decided to use Instagram as their primary marketing tool. Through regular posts featuring their baked goods and stories detailing their baking process, the bakery saw increased footfall and a significant rise in online orders. As their popularity grew, so did their revenues, demonstrating the direct correlation between social media engagement and financial success.

In the tech world, a startup named TechVentures is another shining example. They utilized LinkedIn and Twitter to connect with potential investors and clients. Not only did this strategy lead to increased funding for their business, it also granted them exposure to a wide audience, thereby expanding their clientele and increasing their revenues.

Collectively, these stories weave a tapestry of success illustrating the power of social media in personal and business finance. The platforms of social media, typically seen as tools for communication, entertainment, and networking, when utilized smartly, become channels for gaining financial stability and wealth. The underlying message in these narratives is the immense potential social media holds for transforming personal finance and creating a successful financial future.

www.ingramcontent.com/pod-product-compliance
Lightning Source LLC
Chambersburg PA
CBHW071044260726
48661CB00007B/3153